Seasons

Seasons 123

Patricia Whitehouse

Heinemann Library
Chicago, Illinois

Designed by Sue Emerson, Heinemann Library
Printed and bound in the U.S.A. by Lake Book

07 06 05 04 03
10 9 8 7 6 5 4 3 2 1

Library of Congress Cataloging-in-Publication Data
Whitehouse, Patricia, 1958–
    Seasons 123 / Patricia Whitehouse.
        p. cm. — (Seasons)
Includes index.
Summary: A counting book that features items associated with particular seasons, such as flowers blooming in the spring or snow balls in the winter.
    ISBN: 1-58810-896-1 (HC), 1-40340-538-7 (Pbk.)
    1. Counting—Juvenile literature. 2. Seasons—Juvenile literature. [1. Counting. 2. Seasons.]
    I. Title. II. Seasons
    (Heinemann Library)
    QA113 .W4957 2003
    513.2''11—dc21
                                    2002001171

JJ
EASY
Whitehouse

Acknowledgments
The author and publishers are grateful to the following for permission to reproduce copyright material:
p. 3 Miles Ertman/Masterfile; p. 5 International Stock; p. 7 Charles Gold/Corbis Stock Market; p. 9 J. A. Kraulis/ Masterfile; pp. 11, 22 Scott Braut; p. 13 Darrell Gulin/Stone/Getty Images; p. 15 Bryan Peterson/FPG International/Getty Images; p. 17 Bill Boch/Foodpix; p. 19 Lewis Kemper/Mira.com; p. 21 Ted Horowitz/Corbis Stock Market

Cover photographs (L-R) by Thomas E. Welch/Visuals Unlimited, Inc., Lewis Kemper/Mira.com, Davin Ponton/Getty Images
Photo research by Scott Braut

Every effort has been made to contact copyright holders of any material reproduced in this book. Any omissions will be rectified in subsequent printings if notice is given to the publisher.

Special thanks to our advisory panel for their help in the preparation of this book:

Eileen Day, Preschool Teacher
Chicago, IL

Ellen Dolmetsch, MLS
Wilmington, DE

Kathleen Gilbert,
Second Grade Teacher
Austin, TX

Sandra Gilbert,
Library Media Specialist
Houston, TX

Angela Leeper,
Educational Consultant
North Carolina Department
of Public Instruction
Raleigh, NC

Pam McDonald,
Reading Teacher
Winter Springs, FL

Melinda Murphy,
Library Media Specialist
Houston, TX

Some words are shown in bold, **like this.**
You can find them in the picture glossary on page 23.

One   1

1

Sometimes you can see rainbows after a spring rain.

How many rainbows do you see?

Two 2

You can taste cold ice cream in the hot summer.

How many ice cream cones do you see?

Three 3

You can taste **maple syrup** on pancakes.

It comes from the **sap** of maple trees in spring.

How many pancakes do you see?

1

2

3

Four 4

Winter, spring, summer, and fall are seasons.

How many seasons are in a year?

winter

spring

1

2

3

4

summer

fall

Five 5

You can feel cold snow in the winter.

How many **snowballs** do you see?

1   2   3   4   5

Six   6

You can hear **geese** honking in the fall.

How many geese do you see?

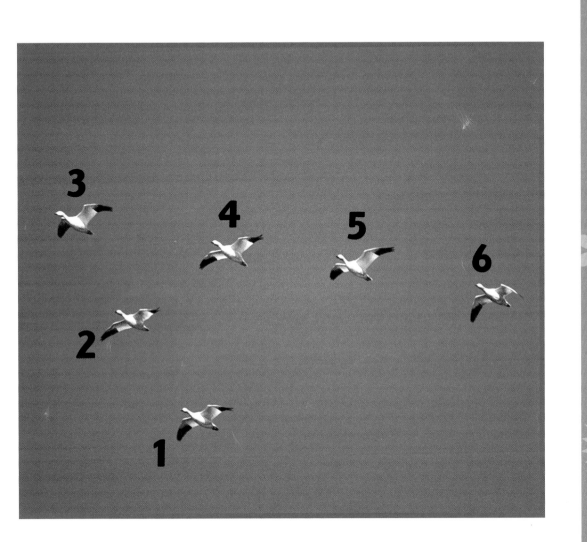

3
2
4
5
6
1

13

Seven 7

Spring rain helps
flowers bloom.

How many tulips
do you see?

Eight 8

You can smell food cooking outside in the summer.

How many hot dogs are on the **grill?**

Nine 9

You can feel dry, crunchy leaves in the fall.

How many leaves do you see?

Ten   10

You can feel hot **sand** on your toes in the summer.

How many sandy toes do you see?

Look Closely!

How many spring flowers can you see here?

Look for the answer on page 24.

Picture Glossary

goose
(more than one
are geese)
page 12

sand
page 20

snowball
page 10

grill
page 16

sap
page 6

tulip
page 15

maple syrup
page 6

Note to Parents and Teachers

Using this book, children can practice basic mathematical skills while learning interesting facts about the seasons. Help children see the relationship between the numerals 1 through 10 and the sun icons at the bottom of each text page. Extend the concept by drawing ten sun icons on a sheet of construction paper. Cut out the paper "suns." Together, read *Seasons 123*, and as you do so, ask the child to place the appropriate number of "suns" on the photograph. This activity can also be done using manipulatives such as dried beans or small plastic beads.

Index

Answer to quiz on page 22
There are 10 spring flowers.